This Gratitude Journal Belongs To:

_____

_____

Date:

_____

_____

_____

Thoughts and Doodles

Today I am Grateful For:

In the same way, let your light shine before men, that they may see your good deeds and praise your Father in heaven. Matt 5:16

My Prayers for Others:

Thoughts and Doodles

Today I am Grateful For:

_____
_____
_____
_____
_____
_____
_____
_____
_____
_____
_____

Jesus replied: 'Love the Lord your God with all your heart and with all your soul and with all your mind.' Matt:22:37

My Prayers for Others:

_____
_____
_____
_____
_____
_____
_____
_____
_____

Thoughts and Doodles

Today I am Grateful For:

Let us then approach the throne of grace
with confidence, so that we may receive
mercy and find grace to help us in our time
of need. Heb:4:16

My Prayers for Others:

Thoughts and Doodles

Today I am Grateful For:

For God did not send his Son into the world to condemn the world, but to save the world through him. John:3:17

My Prayers for Others:

Thoughts and Doodles

Today I am Grateful For:

_____
_____
_____
_____
_____
_____
_____
_____
_____
_____

By this all men will know that you are my
disciples, if you love one another.
John:13:35

My Prayers for Others:

_____
_____
_____
_____
_____
_____
_____
_____

Thoughts and Doodles

Today I am Grateful For:

_____
_____
_____
_____
_____
_____
_____
_____
_____

Neither height nor depth, nor anything else
in all creation, will be able to separate us
from the love of God that is in Christ Jesus
our Lord.Rom:8:39

My Prayers for Others:

_____
_____
_____
_____
_____
_____
_____
_____

Thoughts and Doodles

Today I am Grateful For:

Yet to all who received him, to those who believed in his name, he gave the right to become children of God. John 1:12

My Prayers for Others:

Thoughts and Doodles

Today I am Grateful For:

_____
_____
_____
_____
_____
_____
_____
_____
_____
_____
_____

He has showed you, O man, what is good. And
what does the LORD require of you? To act justly
and to love mercy and to walk humbly with your
God. Mic 6:8

My Prayers for Others:

_____
_____
_____
_____
_____
_____
_____
_____
_____
_____

Thoughts and Doodles

Today I am Grateful For:

This is how we know what love is: Jesus Christ laid down his life for us. And we ought to lay down our lives for our brothers.
1 John 3:16.

My Prayers for Others:

Thoughts and Doodles

Today I am Grateful For:

Therefore confess your sins to each other and pray for each other so that you may be healed. Jas 5:16

My Prayers for Others:

Thoughts and Doodles

Today I am Grateful For:

Therefore, as God's chosen people, holy and dearly loved, clothe yourselves with compassion, kindness, humility, gentleness and patience. Col 3:12

My Prayers for Others:

Thoughts and Doodles

Today I am Grateful For:

_____
_____
_____
_____
_____
_____
_____
_____
_____
_____
_____

May the God of hope fill you with all joy and peace as you trust in him, so that you may overflow with hope by the power of the Holy Spirit.Rom:15:13

My Prayers for Others:

_____
_____
_____
_____
_____
_____
_____
_____
_____
_____

Thoughts and Doodles

Today I am Grateful For:

Jesus said to her, "I am the resurrection and the life. He who believes in me will live, even though he dies. John 11:25

My Prayers for Others:

Thoughts and Doodles

Today I am Grateful For:

Peter replied, "Repent and be baptized, every one of you, in the name of Jesus Christ for the forgiveness of your sins." Acts 2:38

My Prayers for Others:

Thoughts and Doodles

Today I am Grateful For:

For I know the plans I have for you," declares the LORD, "plans to prosper you and not to harm you, plans to give you hope and a future. Jer. 29:11

My Prayers for Others:

Thoughts and Doodles

Today I am Grateful For:

Trust in the LORD with all your heart and
lean not on your own understanding.
Prov 3:5

My Prayers for Others:

Thoughts and Doodles

Today I am Grateful For:

_____
_____
_____
_____
_____
_____
_____
_____
_____
_____

And teaching them to obey everything I have
commanded you. And surely I am with you
always, to the very end of the age.
Matt 28:20

My Prayers for Others:

_____
_____
_____
_____
_____
_____
_____
_____
_____
_____

Thoughts and Doodles

Today I am Grateful For:

_____
_____
_____
_____
_____
_____
_____
_____
_____
_____

But those who hope in the LORD will renew their strength. They will soar on wings like eagles; they will run and not grow weary, they will walk and not be faint. Isa 40:31

My Prayers for Others:

_____
_____
_____
_____
_____
_____
_____
_____
_____
_____

Thoughts and Doodles

Today I am Grateful For:

Now faith is being sure of what we hope for
and certain of what we do not see.
Heb 11:1

My Prayers for Others:

Thoughts and Doodles

Today I am Grateful For:

_____
_____
_____
_____
_____
_____
_____
_____
_____
_____

That if you confess with your mouth, "Jesus is Lord," and believe in your heart that God raised him from the dead, you will be saved.
Rom 10:9

My Prayers for Others:

_____
_____
_____
_____
_____
_____
_____
_____

Thoughts and Doodles

Today I am Grateful For:

Take my yoke upon you and learn from me,
for I am gentle and humble in heart, and you
will find rest for your souls. Matt 11:29

My Prayers for Others:

Thoughts and Doodles

Today I am Grateful For:

Very truly I tell you, the one who believes
has eternal life.
John 6:47

My Prayers for Others:

Thoughts and Doodles

Today I am Grateful For:

Be on your guard; stand firm in the faith; be
courageous; be strong.
1 Corinthians 16:13

My Prayers for Others:

Thoughts and Doodles

Today I am Grateful For:

_____
_____
_____
_____
_____
_____
_____
_____
_____
_____
_____

Do not merely listen to the word, and so
deceive yourselves. Do what it says.
James 1:22

My Prayers for Others:

_____
_____
_____
_____
_____
_____
_____
_____
_____

Thoughts and Doodles

Today I am Grateful For:

Because of the Lord's great love we are not
consumed, for his compassions never fail.
Lam 3:22-23

My Prayers for Others:

Thoughts and Doodles

Today I am Grateful For:

_____
_____
_____
_____
_____
_____
_____
_____
_____
_____

Jesus Christ is the same yesterday and today
and forever.
Hebrews 13:8

My Prayers for Others:

_____
_____
_____
_____
_____
_____
_____
_____
_____

Thoughts and Doodles

Today I am Grateful For:

But the fruit of the Spirit is love, joy, peace, patience, kindness, goodness, faithfulness.
Gal 5:22

My Prayers for Others:

Thoughts and Doodles

Today I am Grateful For:

In all your ways acknowledge him, and he
will make your paths straight.
Prov 3:6

My Prayers for Others:

Thoughts and Doodles

Today I am Grateful For:

Delight yourself in the LORD and he will give
you the desires of your heart.
Ps 37:4

My Prayers for Others:

Thoughts and Doodles

Today I am Grateful For:

How good and pleasant it is when brothers
live together in unity.
Ps 133:1

My Prayers for Others:

Thoughts and Doodles

Today I am Grateful For:

In the beginning was the Word, and the
Word was with God, and the Word was God.
John 1:1

My Prayers for Others:

Thoughts and Doodles

Today I am Grateful For:

_____
_____
_____
_____
_____
_____
_____
_____
_____

Therefore, as God's chosen people, holy and dearly loved, clothe yourselves with compassion, kindness, humility, gentleness and patience. Col 3:12

My Prayers for Others:

_____
_____
_____
_____
_____
_____
_____
_____
_____

Thoughts and Doodles

Today I am Grateful For:

_____
_____
_____
_____
_____
_____
_____
_____
_____

Consider it pure joy, my brothers, whenever
you face trials of many kinds.
Jas 1:2

My Prayers for Others:

_____
_____
_____
_____
_____
_____
_____
_____

Thoughts and Doodles

Today I am Grateful For:

Cast all your anxiety on him because he cares
for you.
1Pet 5:7

My Prayers for Others:

Thoughts and Doodles

Today I am Grateful For:

For we are God's workmanship, created in Christ Jesus to do good works, which God prepared in advance for us to do. Eph 2:10

My Prayers for Others:

Thoughts and Doodles

Today I am Grateful For:

Keep your lives free from the love of money and be content with what you have, because God has said, "Never will I leave you; never will I forsake you." Heb 13:5

My Prayers for Others:

Thoughts and Doodles

Today I am Grateful For:

So do not fear, for I am with you;
do not be dismayed, for I am your God.
Isiah 41:10

My Prayers for Others:

Thoughts and Doodles

Today I am Grateful For:

_____
_____
_____
_____
_____
_____
_____
_____

Be completely humble and gentle; be
patient, bearing with one another in love
Eph 4:2

My Prayers for Others:

_____
_____
_____
_____
_____
_____
_____
_____

Thoughts and Doodles

Today I am Grateful For:

Let the morning bring me word of your unfailing love, for I have put my trust in you Ps 143:8.

My Prayers for Others:

Thoughts and Doodles

Today I am Grateful For:

_____
_____
_____
_____
_____
_____
_____

Love is patient, love is kind. It does not envy,
it does not boast, it is not proud.
Cor 13:4

My Prayers for Others:

_____
_____
_____
_____
_____
_____
_____

Thoughts and Doodles

Today I am Grateful For:

But you, O Lord, are a God merciful and
gracious, slow to anger and abounding in
steadfast love and faithfulness.
Psalm 86:15

My Prayers for Others:

Thoughts and Doodles

Today I am Grateful For:

_____

_____

_____

_____

_____

_____

_____

Be of sober spirit, be on the alert. Your
adversary, the devil, prowls around like a
roaring lion, seeking someone to devour.
1 Pet. 5:81

My Prayers for Others:

_____

_____

_____

_____

_____

_____

_____

Thoughts and Doodles

Today I am Grateful For:

Each man should give what he has decided in
his heart to give, not reluctantly or under
compulsion, for God loves a cheerful giver.
2 Cor. 9:7

My Prayers for Others:

Thoughts and Doodles

Today I am Grateful For:

I will give thanks to you, for I am fearfully and wonderfully made; wonderful are Your works, and my soul knows it very well.
Psalm 139:14

My Prayers for Others:

Thoughts and Doodles

Today I am Grateful For:

_____
_____
_____
_____
_____
_____
_____
_____

Then He told them, The Sabbath was made
for man and not man for the Sabbath.
Mark 2:27

My Prayers for Others:

_____
_____
_____
_____
_____
_____
_____
_____

Thoughts and Doodles

Today I am Grateful For:

Do not be deceived: God cannot be
mocked. A man reaps what he sows.
Galatians 6:7

My Prayers for Others:

Thoughts and Doodles

Today I am Grateful For:

Every word of God proves true; he is a
shield to those who take refuge in him.
Proverbs 30:5

My Prayers for Others:

Thoughts and Doodles

Today I am Grateful For:

Let us think of ways to motivate one another
to acts of love and good works."
Heb10:24

My Prayers for Others:

Thoughts and Doodles

Today I am Grateful For:

_____
_____
_____
_____
_____
_____
_____
_____
_____

Love the LORD your God with all your
heart and with all your soul and with all your
Strength
Deuteronomy 6:5

My Prayers for Others:

_____
_____
_____
_____
_____
_____
_____
_____
_____

Thoughts and Doodles

Today I am Grateful For:

"For he satisfies the thirsty and fills the
hungry with good things."
Psalm 107:9

My Prayers for Others:

Thoughts and Doodles